MOTORCYCLE RIDE JOURNAL

This Log Book Belongs to

_____

FastForwardPublishing.com

ISBN-13: 978-1505673234
ISBN-10: 1505673232

The Ride

Day:_____ Date:_____ Time:_____ Departed

Bike I'm Riding:_____

Starting Mileage:_____ Weather:_____

Leaving From:_____ Going To:_____

☐ Riding Solo   or   ☐ with Others

Friend(s) Along for the Ride:_____

_____

_____

Group Attitude:_____

_____

My Attitude:_____

_____

People I/We Met:_____

_____

Trip Highlights:_____

_____

_____

_____

Best Thing to Happen:_____

_____

Worst Thing to Happen:_____

_____

Accomodations:_____

_____

Restaurants:_____

_____

Ending Mileage:_____ Miles Ridden:_____

Bike Performance □ Excellent   □ Good   □ Poor

Why?_____

_____

Will I do this ride again? □ Yes   □ No   Why? _____

_____

Notes:_____

_____

_____

_____

_____

_____

Notes:_____

_____

_____

_____

_____

_____

_____

_____

_____

_____

_____

_____

_____

_____

_____

_____

_____

_____

_____

_____

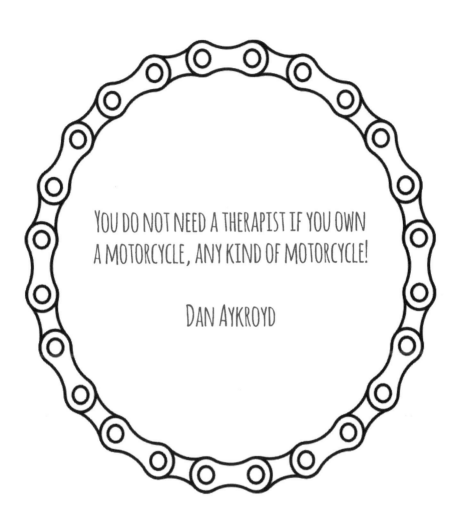

You do not need a therapist if you own a motorcycle, any kind of motorcycle!

Dan Aykroyd

The Ride

Day:_____ Date:_____ Time:_____ Departed

Bike I'm Riding:_____

Starting Mileage:_____ Weather:_____

Leaving From:_____ Going To:_____

☐ Riding Solo   or   ☐ with Others

Friend(s) Along for the Ride:_____

_____

_____

Group Attitude:_____

_____

My Attitude:_____

_____

People I/We Met:_____

_____

Trip Highlights:_____

_____

_____

_____

Best Thing to Happen:_____

_____

Worst Thing to Happen:_____

_____

Accomodations:_____

_____

Restaurants:_____

_____

Ending Mileage:_____ Miles Ridden:_____

Bike Performance □ Excellent   □ Good   □ Poor

Why?_____

_____

Will I do this ride again? □ Yes   □ No Why? _____

_____

Notes:_____

_____

_____

_____

_____

_____

Notes:_____

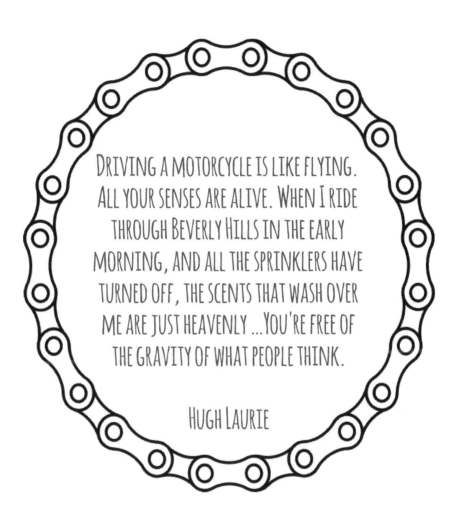

Driving a motorcycle is like flying. All your senses are alive. When I ride through Beverly Hills in the early morning, and all the sprinklers have turned off, the scents that wash over me are just heavenly ...You're free of the gravity of what people think.

Hugh Laurie

The Ride

Day:_____ Date:_____ Time:_____ Departed

Bike I'm Riding:_____

Starting Mileage:_____ Weather:_____

Leaving From:_____ Going To:_____

☐ Riding Solo   or   ☐ with Others

Friend(s) Along for the Ride:_____

_____

_____

Group Attitude:_____

_____

My Attitude:_____

_____

People I/We Met:_____

_____

Trip Highlights:_____

_____

_____

_____

Best Thing to Happen:_____

_____

Worst Thing to Happen:_____

_____

Accomodations:_____

_____

Restaurants:_____

_____

Ending Mileage:_____ Miles Ridden:_____

Bike Performance □ Excellent   □ Good   □ Poor

Why?_____

_____

Will I do this ride again? □ Yes   □ No   Why? _____

_____

Notes:_____

_____

_____

_____

_____

_____

Notes:

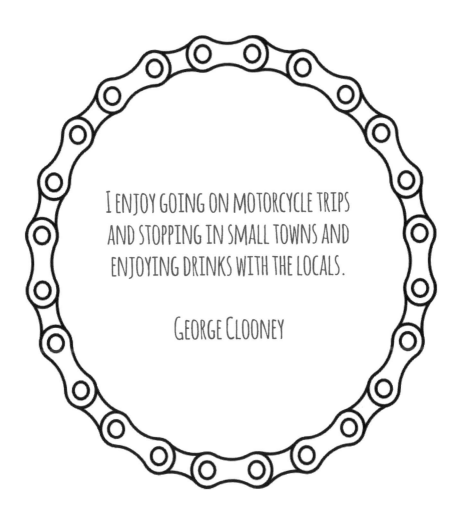

I ENJOY GOING ON MOTORCYCLE TRIPS
AND STOPPING IN SMALL TOWNS AND
ENJOYING DRINKS WITH THE LOCALS.

GEORGE CLOONEY

The Ride

Day:_____ Date:_____ Time:_____ Departed

Bike I'm Riding:_____

Starting Mileage:_____ Weather:_____

Leaving From:_____ Going To:_____

☐ Riding Solo   or   ☐ with Others

Friend(s) Along for the Ride:_____

_____

_____

Group Attitude:_____

_____

My Attitude:_____

_____

People I/We Met:_____

_____

Trip Highlights:_____

_____

_____

_____

Best Thing to Happen:_____

_____

Worst Thing to Happen:_____

_____

Accomodations:_____

_____

Restaurants:_____

_____

Ending Mileage:_____ Miles Ridden:_____

Bike Performance □ Excellent   □ Good   □ Poor

Why?_____

_____

Will I do this ride again? □ Yes   □ No   Why? _____

_____

Notes:_____

_____

_____

_____

_____

_____

Notes:_____

_____

_____

_____

_____

_____

_____

_____

_____

_____

_____

_____

_____

_____

_____

_____

_____

_____

_____

_____

_____

_____

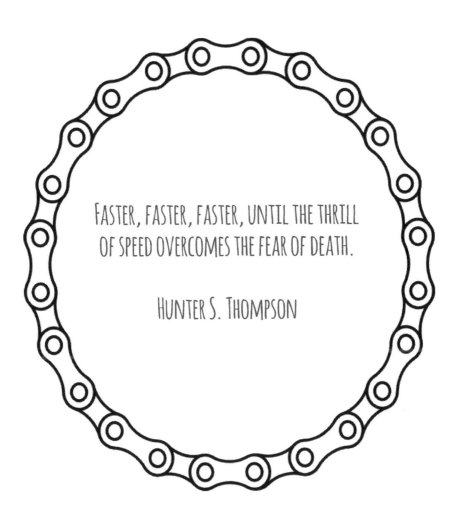

Faster, faster, faster, until the thrill
of speed overcomes the fear of death.

Hunter S. Thompson

The Ride

Day:_____ Date:_____ Time:_____ Departed

Bike I'm Riding:_____

Starting Mileage:_____ Weather:_____

Leaving From:_____ Going To:_____

☐ Riding Solo   or   ☐ with Others

Friend(s) Along for the Ride:_____

_____

_____

Group Attitude:_____

_____

My Attitude:_____

_____

People I/We Met:_____

_____

Trip Highlights:_____

_____

_____

_____

Best Thing to Happen:_____

_____

Worst Thing to Happen:_____

_____

Accomodations:_____

_____

Restaurants:_____

_____

Ending Mileage:_____ Miles Ridden:_____

Bike Performance □ Excellent   □ Good   □ Poor

Why?_____

_____

Will I do this ride again? □ Yes   □ No   Why? _____

_____

Notes:_____

_____

_____

_____

_____

_____

Notes:_____

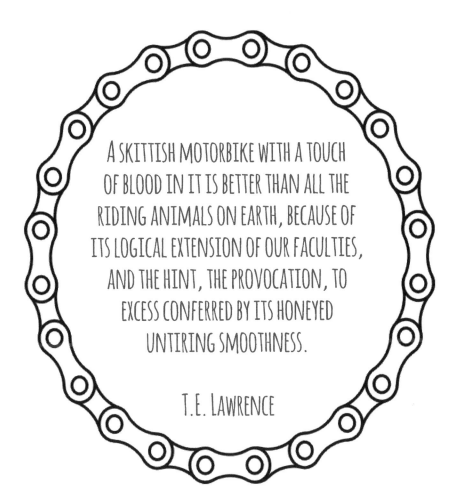

A SKITTISH MOTORBIKE WITH A TOUCH OF BLOOD IN IT IS BETTER THAN ALL THE RIDING ANIMALS ON EARTH, BECAUSE OF ITS LOGICAL EXTENSION OF OUR FACULTIES, AND THE HINT, THE PROVOCATION, TO EXCESS CONFERRED BY ITS HONEYED UNTIRING SMOOTHNESS.

T. E. LAWRENCE

The Ride

Day:_____ Date:_____ Time:_____ Departed

Bike I'm Riding:_____

Starting Mileage:_____ Weather:_____

Leaving From:_____ Going To:_____

☐ Riding Solo   or   ☐ with Others

Friend(s) Along for the Ride:_____

_____

_____

Group Attitude:_____

_____

My Attitude:_____

_____

People I/We Met:_____

_____

Trip Highlights:_____

_____

_____

_____

Best Thing to Happen:_____

_____

Worst Thing to Happen:_____

_____

Accomodations:_____

_____

Restaurants:_____

_____

Ending Mileage:_____ Miles Ridden:_____

Bike Performance □ Excellent   □ Good   □ Poor

Why?_____

_____

Will I do this ride again? □ Yes   □ No   Why? _____

_____

Notes:_____

_____

_____

_____

_____

_____

Notes:_____

I look my best when I take my helmet
off after a long motorcycle ride. I
have a glow and a bit of helmet hair.

Eric Bana

The Ride

Day:_____ Date:_____ Time:_____ Departed

Bike I'm Riding:_____

Starting Mileage:_____ Weather:_____

Leaving From:_____ Going To:_____

☐ Riding Solo   or   ☐ with Others

Friend(s) Along for the Ride:_____

_____

_____

Group Attitude:_____

_____

My Attitude:_____

_____

People I/We Met:_____

_____

Trip Highlights:_____

_____

_____

_____

Best Thing to Happen:_____

_____

Worst Thing to Happen:_____

_____

Accomodations:_____

_____

Restaurants:_____

_____

Ending Mileage:_____ Miles Ridden:_____

Bike Performance □ Excellent   □ Good   □ Poor

Why?_____

_____

Will I do this ride again? □ Yes   □ No   Why? _____

_____

Notes:_____

_____

_____

_____

_____

_____

Notes:_____

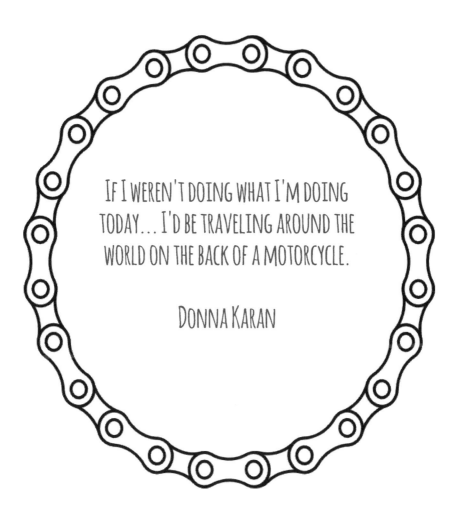

If I weren't doing what I'm doing today... I'd be traveling around the world on the back of a motorcycle.

Donna Karan

The Ride

Day:_____ Date:_____ Time:_____ Departed

Bike I'm Riding:_____

Starting Mileage:_____ Weather:_____

Leaving From:_____ Going To:_____

☐ Riding Solo   or   ☐ with Others

Friend(s) Along for the Ride:_____

_____

_____

Group Attitude:_____

_____

My Attitude:_____

_____

People I/We Met:_____

_____

Trip Highlights:_____

_____

_____

_____

Best Thing to Happen:_____

_____

Worst Thing to Happen:_____

_____

Accomodations:_____

_____

Restaurants:_____

_____

Ending Mileage:_____ Miles Ridden:_____

Bike Performance □ Excellent   □ Good   □ Poor

Why?_____

_____

Will I do this ride again? □ Yes   □ No   Why? _____

_____

Notes:_____

_____

_____

_____

_____

_____

Notes:_____

_____

_____

_____

_____

_____

_____

_____

_____

_____

_____

_____

_____

_____

_____

_____

_____

_____

_____

_____

_____

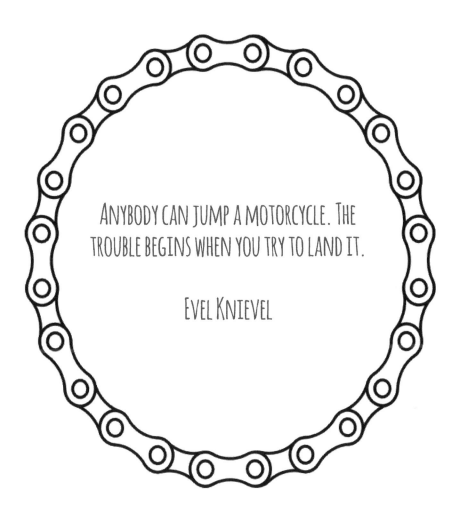

Anybody can jump a motorcycle. The trouble begins when you try to land it.

Evel Knievel

The Ride

Day:_____ Date:_____ Time:_____ Departed

Bike I'm Riding:_____

Starting Mileage:_____ Weather:_____

Leaving From:_____ Going To:_____

☐ Riding Solo   or   ☐ with Others

Friend(s) Along for the Ride:_____

_____

_____

Group Attitude:_____

_____

My Attitude:_____

_____

People I/We Met:_____

_____

Trip Highlights:_____

_____

_____

_____

Best Thing to Happen:_____

_____

Worst Thing to Happen:_____

_____

Accomodations:_____

_____

Restaurants:_____

_____

Ending Mileage:_____ Miles Ridden:_____

Bike Performance □ Excellent   □ Good   □ Poor

Why?_____

_____

Will I do this ride again? □ Yes   □ No   Why? _____

_____

Notes:_____

_____

_____

_____

_____

_____

Notes:_____

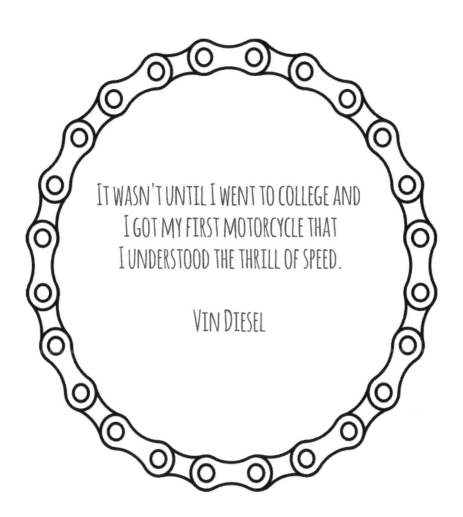

It wasn't until I went to college and
I got my first motorcycle that
I understood the thrill of speed.

Vin Diesel

The Ride

Day:_____ Date:_____ Time:_____ Departed

Bike I'm Riding:_____

Starting Mileage:_____ Weather:_____

Leaving From:_____ Going To:_____

☐ Riding Solo   or   ☐ with Others

Friend(s) Along for the Ride:_____

_____

_____

Group Attitude:_____

_____

My Attitude:_____

_____

People I/We Met:_____

_____

Trip Highlights:_____

_____

_____

_____

Best Thing to Happen:_____

_____

Worst Thing to Happen:_____

_____

Accomodations:_____

_____

Restaurants:_____

_____

Ending Mileage:_____ Miles Ridden:_____

Bike Performance □ Excellent   □ Good   □ Poor

Why?_____

_____

Will I do this ride again? □ Yes   □ No   Why? _____

_____

Notes:_____

_____

_____

_____

_____

_____

Notes:_____

You know, "Motorcycle Diaries" has no incredible stories, no sudden plot twists, it doesn't play that way. It's about recognizing that instance of change and embracing it.

Gael Garcia Bernal

The Ride

Day:_____ Date:_____ Time:_____ Departed

Bike I'm Riding:_____

Starting Mileage:_____ Weather:_____

Leaving From:_____ Going To:_____

☐ Riding Solo   or   ☐ with Others

Friend(s) Along for the Ride:_____

_____

_____

Group Attitude:_____

_____

My Attitude:_____

_____

People I/We Met:_____

_____

Trip Highlights:_____

_____

_____

_____

Best Thing to Happen:_____

_____

Worst Thing to Happen:_____

_____

Accomodations:_____

_____

Restaurants:_____

_____

Ending Mileage:_____ Miles Ridden:_____

Bike Performance □ Excellent   □ Good   □ Poor

Why?_____

_____

Will I do this ride again? □ Yes   □ No   Why? _____

_____

Notes:_____

_____

_____

_____

_____

_____

Notes:_____

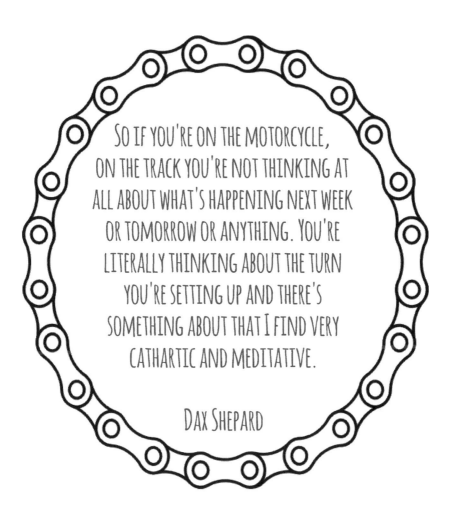

So if you're on the motorcycle, on the track you're not thinking at all about what's happening next week or tomorrow or anything. You're literally thinking about the turn you're setting up and there's something about that I find very cathartic and meditative.

Dax Shepard

The Ride

Day:_____ Date:_____ Time:_____ Departed

Bike I'm Riding:_____

Starting Mileage:_____ Weather:_____

Leaving From:_____ Going To:_____

☐ Riding Solo   or   ☐ with Others

Friend(s) Along for the Ride:_____

_____

_____

Group Attitude:_____

_____

My Attitude:_____

_____

People I/We Met:_____

_____

Trip Highlights:_____

_____

_____

_____

Best Thing to Happen:_____

_____

Worst Thing to Happen:_____

_____

Accomodations:_____

_____

Restaurants:_____

_____

Ending Mileage:_____ Miles Ridden:_____

Bike Performance ☐ Excellent   ☐ Good   ☐ Poor

Why?_____

_____

Will I do this ride again? ☐ Yes   ☐ No   Why? _____

_____

Notes:_____

_____

_____

_____

_____

_____

Notes:_____

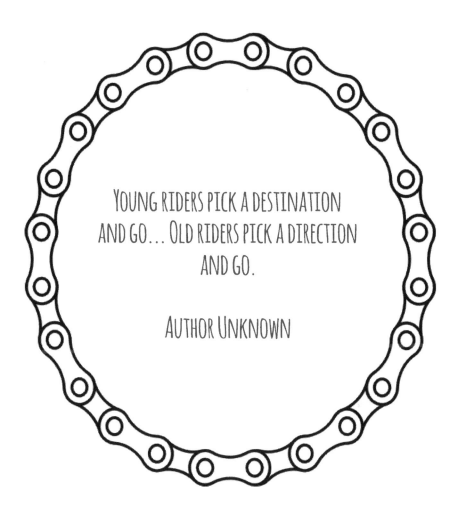

Young riders pick a destination and go… Old riders pick a direction and go.

Author Unknown

The Ride

Day:_____ Date:_____ Time:_____ Departed

Bike I'm Riding:_____

Starting Mileage:_____ Weather:_____

Leaving From:_____ Going To:_____

☐ Riding Solo   or   ☐ with Others

Friend(s) Along for the Ride:_____

_____

_____

Group Attitude:_____

_____

My Attitude:_____

_____

People I/We Met:_____

_____

Trip Highlights:_____

_____

_____

_____

Best Thing to Happen:_____

_____

Worst Thing to Happen:_____

_____

Accomodations:_____

_____

Restaurants:_____

_____

Ending Mileage:_____ Miles Ridden:_____

Bike Performance □ Excellent   □ Good   □ Poor

Why?_____

_____

Will I do this ride again? □ Yes   □ No   Why? _____

_____

Notes:_____

_____

_____

_____

_____

_____

Notes:_____

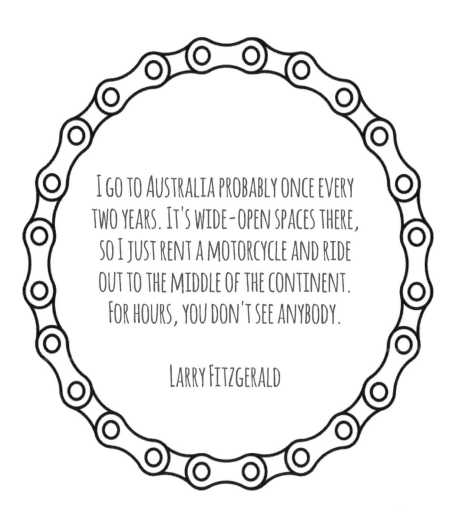

I go to Australia probably once every two years. It's wide-open spaces there, so I just rent a motorcycle and ride out to the middle of the continent. For hours, you don't see anybody.

Larry Fitzgerald

The Ride

Day:_____ Date:_____ Time:_____ Departed

Bike I'm Riding:_____

Starting Mileage:_____ Weather:_____

Leaving From:_____ Going To:_____

☐ Riding Solo   or   ☐ with Others

Friend(s) Along for the Ride:_____

_____

_____

Group Attitude:_____

_____

My Attitude:_____

_____

People I/We Met:_____

_____

Trip Highlights:_____

_____

_____

_____

Best Thing to Happen:_____

_____

Worst Thing to Happen:_____

_____

Accomodations:_____

_____

Restaurants:_____

_____

Ending Mileage:_____ Miles Ridden:_____

Bike Performance □ Excellent   □ Good   □ Poor

Why?_____

_____

Will I do this ride again? □ Yes   □ No   Why? _____

_____

Notes:_____

_____

_____

_____

_____

_____

Notes:_____

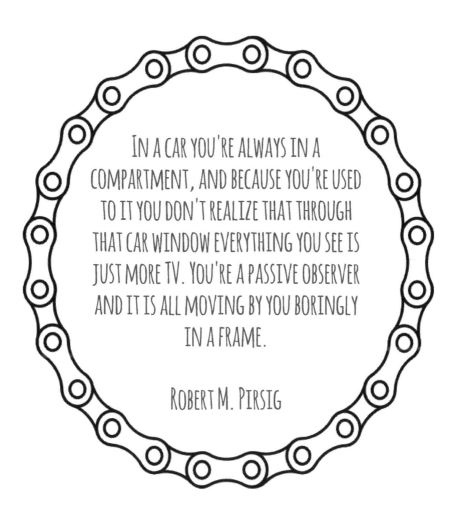

In a car you're always in a compartment, and because you're used to it you don't realize that through that car window everything you see is just more TV. You're a passive observer and it is all moving by you boringly in a frame.

Robert M. Pirsig

The Ride

Day:_____ Date:_____ Time:_____ Departed

Bike I'm Riding:_____

Starting Mileage:_____ Weather:_____

Leaving From:_____ Going To:_____

☐ Riding Solo   or   ☐ with Others

Friend(s) Along for the Ride:_____

_____

_____

Group Attitude:_____

_____

My Attitude:_____

_____

People I/We Met:_____

_____

Trip Highlights:_____

_____

_____

_____

Best Thing to Happen:_____

_____

Worst Thing to Happen:_____

_____

Accomodations:_____

_____

Restaurants:_____

_____

Ending Mileage:_____ Miles Ridden:_____

Bike Performance □ Excellent   □ Good   □ Poor

Why?_____

_____

Will I do this ride again? □ Yes   □ No   Why? _____

_____

Notes:_____

_____

_____

_____

_____

_____

Notes:_____

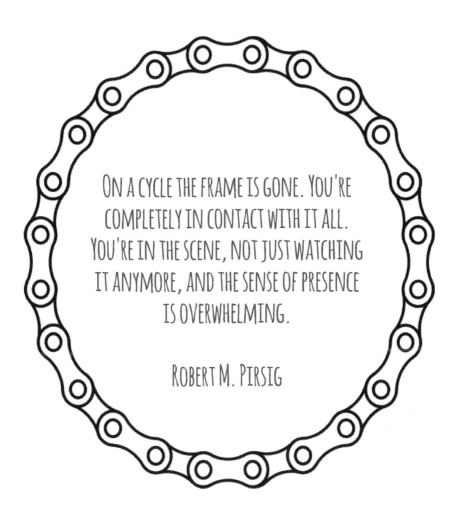

On a cycle the frame is gone. You're completely in contact with it all. You're in the scene, not just watching it anymore, and the sense of presence is overwhelming.

Robert M. Pirsig

The Ride

Day:_____ Date:_____ Time:_____ Departed

Bike I'm Riding:_____

Starting Mileage:_____ Weather:_____

Leaving From:_____ Going To:_____

☐ Riding Solo   or   ☐ with Others

Friend(s) Along for the Ride:_____

_____

_____

Group Attitude:_____

_____

My Attitude:_____

_____

People I/We Met:_____

_____

Trip Highlights:_____

_____

_____

_____

Best Thing to Happen:_____

_____

Worst Thing to Happen:_____

_____

Accomodations:_____

_____

Restaurants:_____

_____

Ending Mileage:_____ Miles Ridden:_____

Bike Performance □ Excellent   □ Good   □ Poor

Why?_____

_____

Will I do this ride again? □ Yes   □ No   Why? _____

_____

Notes:_____

_____

_____

_____

_____

_____

Notes:_____

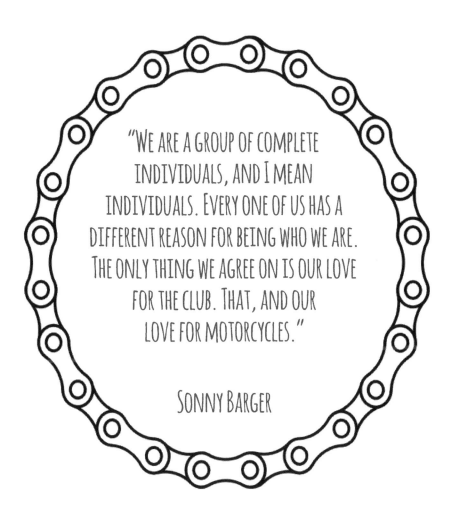

"We are a group of complete individuals, and I mean individuals. Every one of us has a different reason for being who we are. The only thing we agree on is our love for the club. That, and our love for motorcycles."

Sonny Barger

The Ride

Day:_____ Date:_____ Time:_____ Departed

Bike I'm Riding:_____

Starting Mileage:_____ Weather:_____

Leaving From:_____ Going To:_____

☐ Riding Solo   or   ☐ with Others

Friend(s) Along for the Ride:_____

_____

_____

Group Attitude:_____

_____

My Attitude:_____

_____

People I/We Met:_____

_____

Trip Highlights:_____

_____

_____

_____

Best Thing to Happen:_____

_____

Worst Thing to Happen:_____

_____

Accomodations:_____

_____

Restaurants:_____

_____

Ending Mileage:_____ Miles Ridden:_____

Bike Performance □ Excellent   □ Good   □ Poor

Why?_____

_____

Will I do this ride again? □ Yes   □ No   Why? _____

_____

Notes:_____

_____

_____

_____

_____

_____

Notes:_____

_____

_____

_____

_____

_____

_____

_____

_____

_____

_____

_____

_____

_____

_____

_____

_____

_____

_____

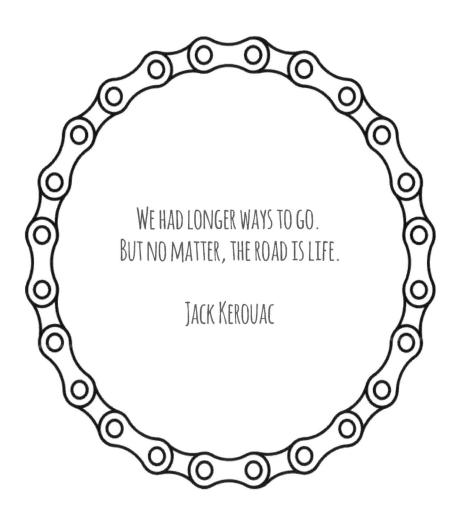

WE HAD LONGER WAYS TO GO.
BUT NO MATTER, THE ROAD IS LIFE.

JACK KEROUAC

The Ride

Day:_____ Date:_____ Time:_____ Departed

Bike I'm Riding:_____

Starting Mileage:_____ Weather:_____

Leaving From:_____ Going To:_____

☐ Riding Solo   or   ☐ with Others

Friend(s) Along for the Ride:_____

_____

_____

Group Attitude:_____

_____

My Attitude:_____

_____

People I/We Met:_____

_____

Trip Highlights:_____

_____

_____

_____

Best Thing to Happen:_____

_____

Worst Thing to Happen:_____

_____

Accomodations:_____

_____

Restaurants:_____

_____

Ending Mileage:_____ Miles Ridden:_____

Bike Performance □ Excellent   □ Good   □ Poor

Why?_____

_____

Will I do this ride again? □ Yes   □ No   Why? _____

_____

Notes:_____

_____

_____

_____

_____

_____

Notes:_____
_____
_____
_____
_____
_____
_____
_____
_____
_____
_____
_____
_____
_____
_____
_____
_____
_____
_____
_____
_____
_____
_____
_____

Sometimes it takes a whole tankful of fuel before you can think straight.

Author Unknown

The Ride

Day:_____ Date:_____ Time:_____ Departed

Bike I'm Riding:_____

Starting Mileage:_____ Weather:_____

Leaving From:_____ Going To:_____

☐ Riding Solo   or   ☐ with Others

Friend(s) Along for the Ride:_____

_____

_____

Group Attitude:_____

_____

My Attitude:_____

_____

People I/We Met:_____

_____

Trip Highlights:_____

_____

_____

_____

Best Thing to Happen:_____

_____

Worst Thing to Happen:_____

_____

Accomodations:_____

_____

Restaurants:_____

_____

Ending Mileage:_____ Miles Ridden:_____

Bike Performance □ Excellent   □ Good   □ Poor

Why?_____

_____

Will I do this ride again? □ Yes   □ No   Why? _____

_____

Notes:_____

_____

_____

_____

_____

_____

Notes:_____

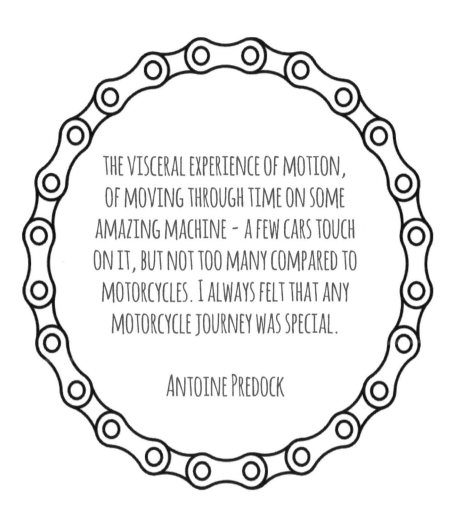

THE VISCERAL EXPERIENCE OF MOTION, OF MOVING THROUGH TIME ON SOME AMAZING MACHINE – A FEW CARS TOUCH ON IT, BUT NOT TOO MANY COMPARED TO MOTORCYCLES. I ALWAYS FELT THAT ANY MOTORCYCLE JOURNEY WAS SPECIAL.

ANTOINE PREDOCK

The Ride

Day:_____ Date:_____ Time:_____ Departed

Bike I'm Riding:_____

Starting Mileage:_____ Weather:_____

Leaving From:_____ Going To:_____

☐ Riding Solo   or   ☐ with Others

Friend(s) Along for the Ride:_____

_____

_____

Group Attitude:_____

_____

My Attitude:_____

_____

People I/We Met:_____

_____

Trip Highlights:_____

_____

_____

_____

Best Thing to Happen:_____

_____

Worst Thing to Happen:_____

_____

Accomodations:_____

_____

Restaurants:_____

_____

Ending Mileage:_____ Miles Ridden:_____

Bike Performance □ Excellent   □ Good   □ Poor

Why?_____

_____

Will I do this ride again? □ Yes   □ No   Why? _____

_____

Notes:_____

_____

_____

_____

_____

_____

Notes:_____

All girls like guys who are tough. Obviously, riding a motorcycle - I don't want to say that there's a bad boy quality - but there's definitely a tough and macho thing about a guy who rides a motorcycles and that element of danger. That's really sexy.

Marisa Miller

The Ride

Day:_____ Date:_____ Time:_____ Departed

Bike I'm Riding:_____

Starting Mileage:_____ Weather:_____

Leaving From:_____ Going To:_____

☐ Riding Solo   or   ☐ with Others

Friend(s) Along for the Ride:_____

_____

_____

Group Attitude:_____

_____

My Attitude:_____

_____

People I/We Met:_____

_____

Trip Highlights:_____

_____

_____

_____

Best Thing to Happen:_____

_____

Worst Thing to Happen:_____

_____

Accomodations:_____

_____

Restaurants:_____

_____

Ending Mileage:_____ Miles Ridden:_____

Bike Performance □ Excellent   □ Good   □ Poor

Why?_____

_____

Will I do this ride again? □ Yes   □ No   Why? _____

_____

Notes:_____

_____

_____

_____

_____

_____

Notes:_____

_____

_____

_____

_____

_____

_____

_____

_____

_____

_____

_____

_____

_____

_____

_____

_____

_____

_____

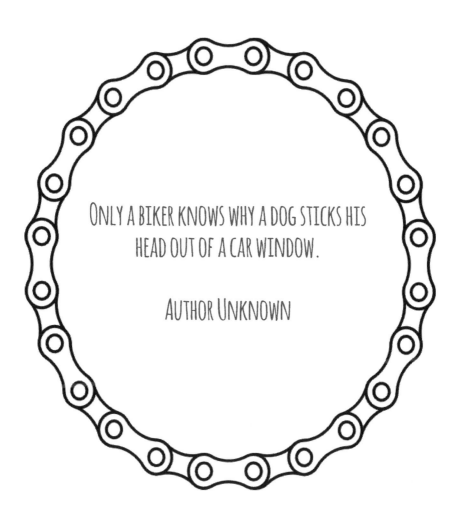

Only a biker knows why a dog sticks his head out of a car window.

Author Unknown

The Ride

Day:_____ Date:_____ Time:_____ Departed

Bike I'm Riding:_____

Starting Mileage:_____ Weather:_____

Leaving From:_____ Going To:_____

☐ Riding Solo   or   ☐ with Others

Friend(s) Along for the Ride:_____

_____

_____

Group Attitude:_____

_____

My Attitude:_____

_____

People I/We Met:_____

_____

Trip Highlights:_____

_____

_____

_____

Best Thing to Happen:_____

_____

Worst Thing to Happen:_____

_____

Accomodations:_____

_____

Restaurants:_____

_____

Ending Mileage:_____ Miles Ridden:_____

Bike Performance ☐ Excellent ☐ Good ☐ Poor

Why?_____

_____

Will I do this ride again? ☐ Yes ☐ No Why? _____

_____

Notes:_____

_____

_____

_____

_____

_____

Notes:_____

_____

_____

_____

_____

_____

_____

_____

_____

_____

_____

_____

_____

_____

_____

_____

_____

_____

_____

_____

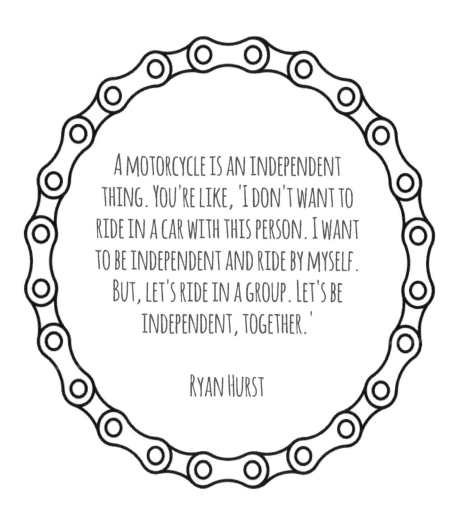

A MOTORCYCLE IS AN INDEPENDENT
THING. YOU'RE LIKE, 'I DON'T WANT TO
RIDE IN A CAR WITH THIS PERSON. I WANT
TO BE INDEPENDENT AND RIDE BY MYSELF.
BUT, LET'S RIDE IN A GROUP. LET'S BE
INDEPENDENT, TOGETHER.'

RYAN HURST

The Ride

Day:_____ Date:_____ Time:_____ Departed

Bike I'm Riding:_____

Starting Mileage:_____ Weather:_____

Leaving From:_____ Going To:_____

☐ Riding Solo   or   ☐ with Others

Friend(s) Along for the Ride:_____

_____

_____

Group Attitude:_____

_____

My Attitude:_____

_____

People I/We Met:_____

_____

Trip Highlights:_____

_____

_____

_____

Best Thing to Happen:_____

_____

Worst Thing to Happen:_____

_____

Accomodations:_____

_____

Restaurants:_____

_____

Ending Mileage:_____ Miles Ridden:_____

Bike Performance □ Excellent   □ Good   □ Poor

Why?_____

_____

Will I do this ride again? □ Yes   □ No   Why? _____

_____

Notes:_____

_____

_____

_____

_____

_____

Notes:_____
_____
_____
_____
_____
_____
_____
_____
_____
_____
_____
_____
_____
_____
_____
_____
_____
_____
_____
_____

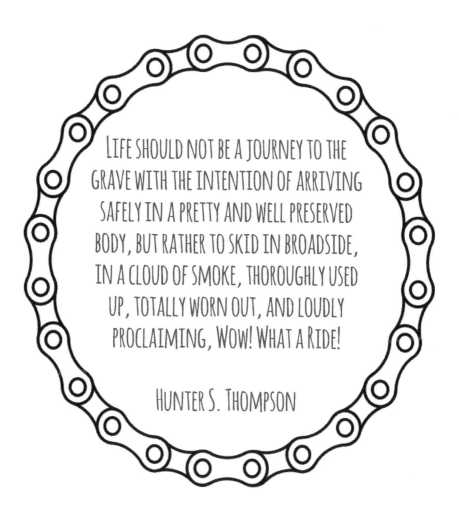

LIFE SHOULD NOT BE A JOURNEY TO THE GRAVE WITH THE INTENTION OF ARRIVING SAFELY IN A PRETTY AND WELL PRESERVED BODY, BUT RATHER TO SKID IN BROADSIDE, IN A CLOUD OF SMOKE, THOROUGHLY USED UP, TOTALLY WORN OUT, AND LOUDLY PROCLAIMING, WOW! WHAT A RIDE!

HUNTER S. THOMPSON

The Ride

Day:_____ Date:_____ Time:_____ Departed

Bike I'm Riding:_____

Starting Mileage:_____ Weather:_____

Leaving From:_____ Going To:_____

☐ Riding Solo   or   ☐ with Others

Friend(s) Along for the Ride:_____

_____

_____

Group Attitude:_____

_____

My Attitude:_____

_____

People I/We Met:_____

_____

Trip Highlights:_____

_____

_____

_____

Best Thing to Happen:_____

_____

Worst Thing to Happen:_____

_____

Accomodations:_____

_____

Restaurants:_____

_____

Ending Mileage:_____ Miles Ridden:_____

Bike Performance ☐ Excellent   ☐ Good   ☐ Poor

Why?_____

_____

Will I do this ride again? ☐ Yes   ☐ No   Why? _____

_____

Notes:_____

_____

_____

_____

_____

_____

Notes:_____

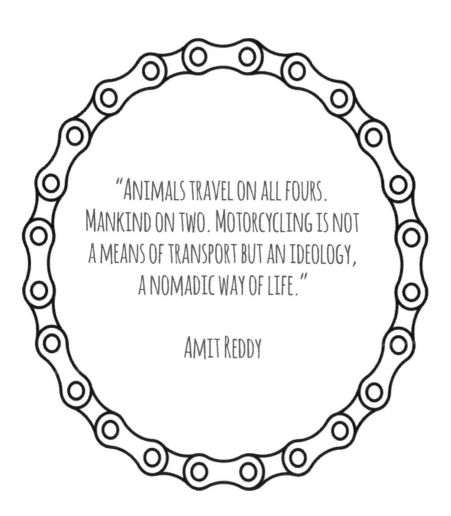

"Animals travel on all fours. Mankind on two. Motorcycling is not a means of transport but an ideology, a nomadic way of life."

Amit Reddy

The Ride

Day:_____ Date:_____ Time:_____ Departed

Bike I'm Riding:_____

Starting Mileage:_____ Weather:_____

Leaving From:_____ Going To:_____

☐ Riding Solo   or   ☐ with Others

Friend(s) Along for the Ride:_____

_____

_____

Group Attitude:_____

_____

My Attitude:_____

_____

People I/We Met:_____

_____

Trip Highlights:_____

_____

_____

_____

Best Thing to Happen:_____

_____

Worst Thing to Happen:_____

_____

Accomodations:_____

_____

Restaurants:_____

_____

Ending Mileage:_____ Miles Ridden:_____

Bike Performance □ Excellent   □ Good   □ Poor

Why?_____

_____

Will I do this ride again? □ Yes   □ No   Why? _____

_____

Notes:_____

_____

_____

_____

_____

_____

Notes:_____

_____

_____

_____

_____

_____

_____

_____

_____

_____

_____

_____

_____

_____

_____

_____

_____

_____

_____

_____

_____

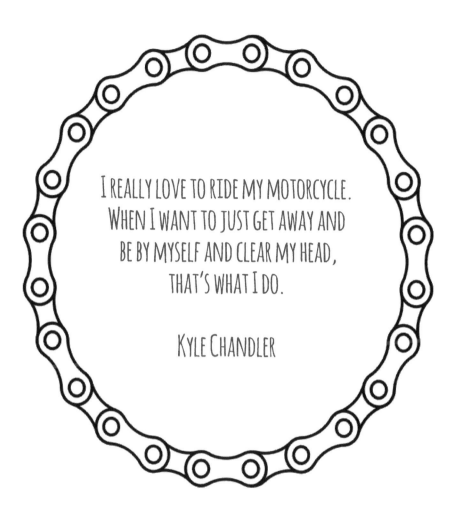

I REALLY LOVE TO RIDE MY MOTORCYCLE.
WHEN I WANT TO JUST GET AWAY AND
BE BY MYSELF AND CLEAR MY HEAD,
THAT'S WHAT I DO.

KYLE CHANDLER

Motorcycle Log Books
Make Great Presents

Here are some of our other cover designs,
all available at Amazon.com and other retailers.

FastForwardPublishing.com

FastForwardPublishing.com

Made in the USA
Middletown, DE
01 August 2015